AUTUMN
A·C·R·O·S·S
AMERICA

SEYMOUR SIMON

HYPERION BOOKS FOR CHILDREN
NEW YORK

This book is dedicated
to those who treasure the natural places across our land.
They leave nothing but footsteps
and take nothing but photographs and memories.

PHOTO CREDITS
Front jacket, back jacket, pp. 5, 9, 22–23, 29 © Seymour Simon; pp. 1, 2–
3 © Barbara Gerlach/Dembinsky Photo Associates; pp. 6–7 © Michael
Baytoff; pp. 10, 30–31, 32 © Lewis Kemper; pp. 12–13, 24 © Stan Oso-
linski/Dembinsky Photo Associates; pp. 14, 15, 16 © Skip Moody/
Dembinsky Photo Associates; p. 19 © Dan Dempster/Dembinsky Photo
Associates; pp. 20–21 © Ron Goulet/Dembinsky Photo Associates; pp.
26–27 © Kathleen Marie Menke/Crystal Images.

Text © 1993 by Seymour Simon.
All rights reserved. Printed in Hong Kong.
For information address Hyperion Books for Children,
114 Fifth Avenue, New York, New York 10011.
FIRST EDITION
1 3 5 7 9 10 8 6 4 2
Library of Congress Cataloging-in-Publication Data

Simon, Seymour.
Autumn across America/Seymour Simon—1st ed.
p. cm.
Summary: Describes the signs of autumn that are seen in different
parts of the United States, such as leaves changing color, migration
of birds and insects, harvesting of crops, and changes in weather.
ISBN 1-56282-467-8 (trade)—ISBN 1-56282-468-6 (lib. bdg.)
1. Autumn—United States—Juvenile literature. 2. Fall foliage—
United States—Juvenile literature. [1. Autumn. 2. United
States—Description and travel.] I. Title.
QH81.S613 1993
508.73—dc20 92-55043 CIP AC

This book is set in 16-point Leamington.

Autumn across America is a season of memory and change. In early autumn the days can still be warm and summery, tree leaves still green, insects and birds still active. But as the season advances, daytime grows shorter, darkness comes earlier, and the nights grow colder. Green leaves change to shades of red and yellow, and the colors race from tree to tree like flames in a forest fire. Later, the leaves will fall from the trees and flutter down to the ground in swirling drifts that crackle underfoot.

Autumn is harvesttime for apples and pears, nuts and berries, pumpkins and squash. It is the season for wild plants to release countless seeds that will lie protected in their coats during the cold months of winter and sprout when the warmer days of spring return. Autumn is when insects lay their eggs, squirrels store food, and birds fly south. Autumn is a time for remembering that the seasons follow a great cycle in their changing and always come back to where they were.

The seasons change because of the way Earth's axis is tilted, not because it's closer to the sun in warm weather. In fact, Earth is actually closer to the sun when winter begins in the Northern Hemisphere than it is when summer begins.

Earth spins, or rotates, on its axis, an imaginary line that runs through the North and South Poles. One spin of Earth on its axis makes one day. The axis is tilted a little to one side, at an angle of 23.5°. For every 365 times Earth spins on its axis, it also completes one revolution around the sun, what we call a year. When the North Pole is tilted toward the sun, the Northern Hemisphere has summer. At that time the South Pole is tilted away from the sun, so the Southern Hemisphere has winter. Autumn is the season of change from summer to winter.

The official first day of autumn, on or about September 23, is called the autumnal equinox. An equinox is when day and night are most nearly equal in length. But the autumn season as we think of it in America begins when leaves in northern states begin to change color by September and October.

In the Northeast along the Canadian border, deciduous trees begin their magnificent display of color during August and September. The brilliant yellows, flaming reds, and dazzling oranges sweep southward into New England and the Middle Atlantic states as autumn progresses. Deciduous trees are those that shed their leaves at the end of the growing season. Autumn is often called "fall" because of the falling leaves.

The forests of birches, the aspens and the poplars that cover the hills and mountains, and the sycamores that grow along the banks of streams all change from green to shades of yellow early in the season. American beech brightens into a luminous gold; sassafras and American mountain ash become glowing orange. Yellows are the most common leaf colors, but reds are perhaps the most brilliant.

Across the valleys and the hills of New England, sugar maples become red, orange, and gold. Sumacs turn fiery scarlet; poison ivy leaves become a richer bronze red. By the middle of October, oaks change from green to yellow-orange or bronze. Most often in the Northeast, the blazing colors are all mixed together, as in this October view of the Catskill Mountains of New York State.

Yellows, oranges, and golds are produced in leaves by pigments (coloring materials) called carotenes, reds by pigments called anthocyanins. You can't see these colors during the growing season because they are hidden by the bright green of chlorophyll. Chlorophyll is the green pigment that helps plant cells use sunlight to make food, a process called photosynthesis. In autumn, as days grow shorter, chlorophyll production slows down and the green fades, revealing the yellows of the carotenes.

When chlorophyll production stops, a layer of woody cells develops and begins to seal off the leaf from the twig. Water can no longer reach the leaf. As the trapped sugar breaks down, red anthocyanin colors are produced by exposure to sunlight. Cloudy, rainy autumn weather prevents the red colors from forming. Ideal red colors come when autumn has bright sunny days followed by cool nights.

In early autumn, thousands upon thousands of snow geese take to the air in a twenty-five-hundred-mile journey from their breeding grounds in the eastern Canadian Arctic to wintering grounds in Middle Atlantic states from New Jersey to North Carolina. By midautumn, the geese begin arriving along the Atlantic coast in flocks of several dozen to several hundred. The greatest number arrive in November, when as many as one million birds may be found in coastal salt marshes from New Jersey to Delaware. If the weather stays mild, huge flocks will remain all winter, but a hard freeze will drive the birds farther south.

The snow geese mix with many other kinds of migratory waterfowl, including Canada, blue, and brant geese; pond ducks such as mallards, black ducks, green-winged teals, pintails, and widgeons; and scaups, mergansers, and other diving ducks.

Important to the survival of these birds are the more than four hundred fifty national wildlife refuges (NWRs) located all over the United States from Florida to Alaska. More than two dozen NWRs in the Middle Atlantic states offer safe nesting and feeding grounds in heavily populated areas. Without these refuges it would be difficult for huge flocks of birds, such as these snow geese along the Jersey Shore, to survive their annual southern migration.

Across the Midwest there seem to be as many insects in early autumn as there are during the height of summer. Clusters of flies and gnats dance in the sunlight, crickets serenade the night, and cicadas take up the insect chorus during the day. But as the days become shorter and cooler, insects gradually begin to disappear.

Beetles, termites, and other ground-dwelling insects migrate, not north to south like birds, but up to down. They go from above ground to protected places beneath logs and rocks, or they burrow deep within the soil. Water-dwelling insects migrate from above the water to below it, or they travel from shallow to deep water.

For many other insects, getting ready for winter means entering a different life stage. Some, such as the praying mantis, lay their eggs in a protective egg case and then die. The eggs stay the winter and hatch in the spring.

The woolly bear caterpillar is the larval stage of a tiger moth. In autumn it spins a protective cocoon of silk and attaches itself to a twig or leaf. Inside the cocoon, the larval caterpillar becomes a pupa. The pupa is motionless, but its body tissues are changing, and in the spring it will emerge as an adult moth.

Autumn is the season when plants produce and scatter seeds far afield. Seeds are life packages for future generations. They contain an embryo, or young plant, and a supply of food. Most seeds are also enclosed in a protective coat that safeguards them during the harsh winter weather so they can sprout in the spring.

Seeds are travelers. Some are hitchhikers and are covered by burs that stick to clothing and the fur of animals that brush against them. These seeds have descriptive names such as sticktights, beggarticks, catchweed, and gripgrass. Other seeds are found in pulpy fruits such as cherries and blueberries. The fruits are eaten by birds, squirrels, and other animals, and then the seeds are voided in distant places. Still other seeds are shot from ripening seedpods such as jewelweed, or drop whirling to the ground like winged maple or elm seeds.

But perhaps the most beautiful autumn seeds come from the common milkweed plants that grow in open meadows and vacant lots. Within a milkweed pod are rows of golden brown seeds, each with a tuft of silken threads. When a pod splits open in October, only a few seeds at a time are released. Their silken parachutes catch the faintest breeze, and they sail off to unknown destinations.

Autumn is not only a time for scattering but also the traditional time when farmers gather their crops. Corn and wheat, grapes and pears, vegetables and nuts, and even fall flowers are harvested in abundance across the country. A dozen different kinds of apples, with names such as Red Delicious, McIntosh, Granny Smith, and Northern Spy, are regularly harvested in apple orchards across the country.

The first full moon after the autumnal equinox is called the harvest moon. When the harvest moon rises, it moves at an angle close to the horizon, behind the dark shadows of trees, hills, and buildings. Compared to these familiar shapes, the harvest moon looks enormous. Because of pollen and other dust particles in the air, the moon often takes on strange shades of orange and red and resembles a huge pumpkin in the sky.

Of all the American harvest, pumpkins may be the one plant most associated with autumn. These brightly colored gourds grow on plant vines that stretch along the ground for thirty feet. Giant pumpkins may weigh as much as two hundred pounds each. Of course, we eat pumpkin pie and pumpkin seeds. But we also make jack-o'-lanterns from pumpkins, and without those funny, lighted orange faces how could we have Halloween?

All across the Midwest and along this country road in Upper Michigan, leaves fall to the ground in late October and early November. Leaf color varies a great deal from place to place and year to year. Within a grove of trees, one or two may show much brighter colors than the rest, whereas other trees simply go brown. Droughts and insect damage can result in a poor leaf display in the autumn. An unusually warm October is also bad for color, since each night the trees use most of the sugar produced in their leaves, so not enough sugar is left for color to develop.

Frost is mainly responsible for freeing the leaves from the trees. On a cold night, ice crystals form and break the woody fibers that hold the leaf to the twig. Then when the ice melts in the early morning sun, the leaves whirl to the ground in a shower of reds, yellows, and browns.

On the ground, the colorful pigments break down, and all the leaves turn an autumnal brown. But the fallen leaves are not wasted in nature. They provide food and shelter for a host of insects and other small animals. They also provide food for mushrooms and other fungi that lack chlorophyll and cannot make their own food. Finally, the leaves decay and their minerals return to the soil, helping to make it more fertile for future plant generations.

In late autumn, many animals live in and about the hot springs and geysers found in Yellowstone National Park. Even in the coldest weather, insects, snails, and fish remain active in the warmed rivers and streams in Yellowstone. Birds, elk, moose, bear, and bison also gather near the warm waters as autumn grows colder.

Yellowstone has about two hundred active geysers. The park sits atop a huge collapsed volcano that still provides underground heat. A geyser erupts when its reservoir of trapped water is heated above the boiling point and suddenly turns to steam, ejecting hot water and steam through a vent to the surface. A complete geyser cycle may take minutes, hours, days, or even years.

At one time, millions of bison migrated south across the American plains every autumn. Native Americans ate their meat and used their hides to make clothing and tepees. The bison was also important in their rituals and religious beliefs. But the settlers who moved west viewed the bison as a nuisance. They killed them in huge numbers, and by 1890, only a few hundred bison were left. Several years later, bison were protected by the federal government. Nowadays, thousands of bison live in preserves and ranches, and several herds live in Yellowstone National Park.

If red and yellow are the main colors of autumn in the East, then yellow and dark green are the main colors of autumn in the mountains and hills of the West. On mountains and hillsides, you often see a grove of bright yellow quaking aspens cutting through a forest of dark green spruce and fir trees like a slash of golden light. Quaking aspens get their name from their oval leaves that shake even in gentle breezes. Aspens belong to a family of deciduous trees called poplars. Poplars are found throughout most of America.

Spruce, fir, pine, hemlock, cedar, and juniper are all members of a group of nonflowering trees called conifers. These trees are common all across America but are particularly common in the mountains and foothills of the Rockies. Conifers are sometimes called evergreens because they do not drop their leaves during any particular season. Conifers have narrow leaves (called needles) that expose a far smaller surface than do leaves of broadleaf trees. Less surface area, along with a waxy coating on their needles, helps reduce conifer water loss in winter. Because conifers keep their leaves year-round, they remain active and grow as soon as there is enough light and the temperature becomes warm enough, typically in the low 50s °F.

Every autumn beginning in October and lasting until December, three thousand or more bald eagles gather in small groups along several miles of the Chilkat River in the Alaska Chilkat Bald Eagle Preserve. This is the largest known gathering of bald eagles anywhere in the world.

The attraction for the eagles is food. An autumn run of ten-pound salmon swim up the river to spawn and die. It is the last salmon run of the season, and eagles flock to the river from hundreds of miles around. Warm, upwelling water keeps parts of the Chilkat from freezing until late in the season. Eagles wade into the water, stab sharp talons into dead or dying salmon, and drag them onto land to feast on the rich meat.

Bald eagles can dive at one hundred miles per hour and spot a fish in a river from a mile away. This majestic bird became the national symbol for the United States in 1782. At one time bald eagles were common all across North America. Now they are on the Endangered Species List in forty-three of the lower forty-eight states because of pesticides, illegal shooting, and habitat destruction. All the more reason that, in 1982, Alaska declared a forty-eight-thousand-acre stretch of the Chilkat River and its surroundings a permanent preserve for the birds.

On the western side of the Olympic Mountains in Washington State, late autumn is a season of heavy rains. Rising from sea level to as high as eight thousand feet, the Olympics present a giant rock barrier against moisture-laden winds off the ocean. The sea winds rush up the mountain slopes, cool suddenly, and drop their moisture as rain. At this time of year, the rain can last for days, and the mists never let up. About 145 inches of rain fall every year, roughly two billion gallons of water for each square mile of land, more rainfall than any other place in America. Yet only forty miles to the west on the other side of the mountains is the driest region north of southern California, with a yearly rainfall of less than 17 inches.

Towering Douglas firs, Sitka spruces, and western hemlocks draped with shaggy mosses and green ferns grow near one another in the valleys of the western Olympics. A green carpet interweaved with dozens of different kinds of mosses covers the ground. Small trees grow atop "nurse logs," fallen trees that decay and create soil beds in which seedlings take root. Vine and bigleaf maples turn red and yellow and drop their leaves in the autumn, but the rain forest of mostly conifer trees remains green and wet. Similar temperate rain forests grow on the Pacific coast from Alaska to California, but the Olympic rain forest is the largest in North America.

All across America, monarch butterflies begin their autumn migrations when temperatures begin to drop. The black-and-orange insects wing their way south across the beaches of the East Coast, over the Appalachians, along the flat farmlands of the Midwest, and even across the great deserts of the Southwest.

The monarch is a good flier, moving from ten to fifteen miles per hour, traveling eighty miles or more in a day. Some monarchs migrate as far as eighteen hundred miles from the north to the south. They will spend the winter in large groups in gathering spots in Florida, Texas, and California.

In Pacific Grove at the southern end of Monterey Bay in California, the monarchs begin arriving in huge numbers in mid-October. They cluster together on trunks and large branches by the thousands and tens of thousands. Their wings folded, most of the butterflies hang motionless, packed closely together, looking like clumps of gray-brown leaves. The monarchs stay about five months. In March, the surviving adults, along with some of their offspring born in the surrounding area, will migrate back to northern breeding areas.

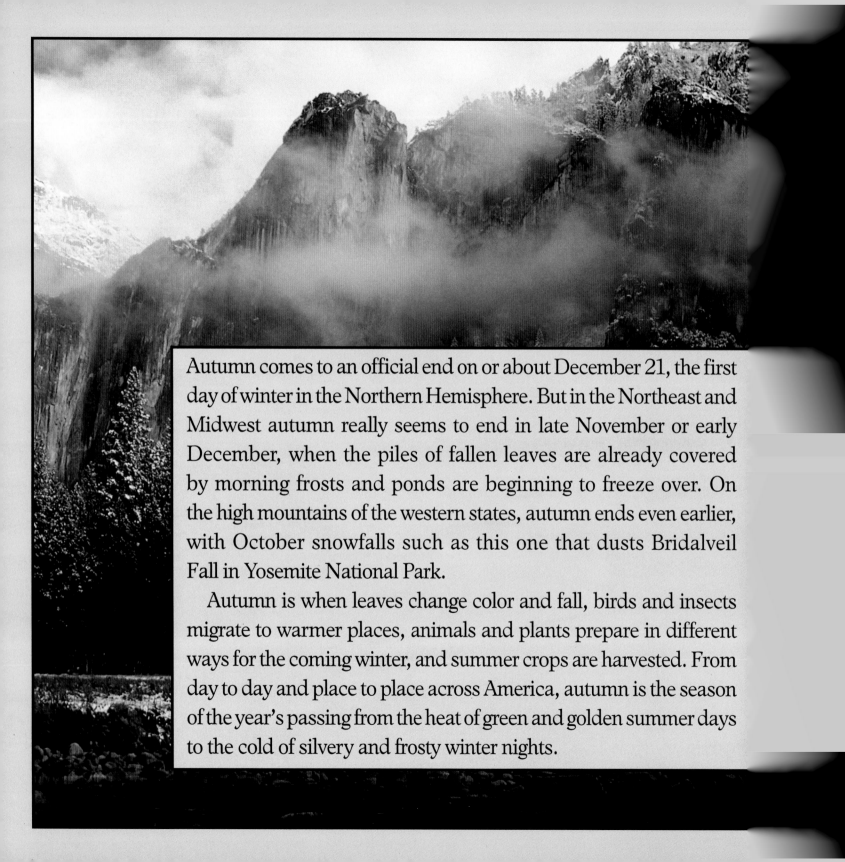

Autumn comes to an official end on or about December 21, the first
day of winter in the Northern Hemisphere. But in the Northeast and
Midwest autumn really seems to end in late November or early
December, when the piles of fallen leaves are already covered
by morning frosts and ponds are beginning to freeze over. On
the high mountains of the western states, autumn ends even earlier,
with October snowfalls such as this one that dusts Bridalveil
Fall in Yosemite National Park.

   Autumn is when leaves change color and fall, birds and insects
migrate to warmer places, animals and plants prepare in different
ways for the coming winter, and summer crops are harvested. From
day to day and place to place across America, autumn is the season
of the year's passing from the heat of green and golden summer days
to the cold of silvery and frosty winter nights.